Endorsements

Betty helps you boldly declare, "Actually, I brought my own shoes" as you reset the standard for excellence whenever you step into a new role. It's important to step into the shoes that fit you. Shoes that are too big will cause you to stumble and shoes that are too tight will bring unnecessary pain. You are unique and no one can be the BEST you!

Byline: Southern California Real Estate Professional and Faith-Based author of two books: *Chosen by God Overlooked by Man: Women of Faith Moving in the Supernatural Gifts of God* and *Hope in the Wilderness: A Faith Guide Through Stormy Seasons* both found on Amazon.com

~Yolanda Dawson, Ed.D

"I watched as Betty transformed into Bessie Coleman. Bessie was a pioneer for women and African American men in the field of aviation. She was an icon. Betty's book will inspire you whether you are a man or a woman, to take the necessary steps to be a pioneer and blaze trails within your sphere of influence. This book is a must-read for anyone desiring to make an impact in their world, whether or not it is on an iconic level."

~Bishop Kelly R. Woods
Chairman, Northern California District Council
Pentecostal Assemblies of the World

Betty encourages the individual who hears, "You've got big shoes to fill," to confidently step into their new role, align themselves to do and become everything they dreamed of, and blaze their own trail.

~Dawn Baker

Betty lets us know it is possible for every person who has been subjected to the subtle rejection that comes from hearing, "You've got big shoes to fill" as they step into a new role, to arise and confidently align themselves with the person God created them to be. The hidden secret about this book is that it is a deliverance manual for the workplace.

~Aldane Walters
Social Media Content Manager

In *Big Shoes to Fill, How to Establish Your Own Brand When Following in the Footsteps of An Icon,* Betty gives the tools one needs to boldly step into a new position with confidence knowing that you will be successful. If you follow the steps Betty gives you, the God-given talents that have been locked away will be unleashed and you will be amazed to discover what was inside of you all along! A must-read!

~Pamela S.

When Betty asked me to do some initial editing for her, I was happy to do it. As I began reading, when it comes to editing, normally you're mainly scanning words, looking for punctuation, sentence clarity, and syntax errors. I was doing that, but I began intentionally reading what was written. I thought, "This is really good." I was loving it and took away many nuggets from what I read. I didn't think the book would be bad, but I was very pleasantly surprised by what I was reading. One word I would use to describe this book is "practical." You will be able to put into action the information provided.

~Rhonda Roberts
Technical Writer

A HUGE THANK YOU to Betty for the incredible coaching session! I was able to get more tasks done in a week and prepare for an important exam. Thank you so much and blessings and love to you! Thank you for being a trailblazer!

~Carol Jones
Financial Planning Assistant
Urban Wealth Management

Big Shoes To Fill

Big Shoes To Fill

How To Establish Your Own Brand When Following In The Footsteps Of An Icon

BETTY JEWELL SLATER

Copyright © 2022 by Betty Jewell Slater

All rights reserved

All rights reserved. No part of this publication may be reproduced, stored in a retrieval system, or transmitted in any form or by any means–for example, electronic, photocopy, and recording—without the prior written permission of the publisher. The only exception is brief quotations in printed reviews.

Paperback: 978-1-64085-507-6
Hardback: 978-1-64085-508-3
Ebook: 978-1-64085-509-0

Library of Congress Control Number (LCCN): 2018965120
Author Academy Elite, Powell, OH

Scripture references are from the King James Version of the Bible

Dedication

This book is dedicated to my son, William Patrick, and my mother, Betty L. Slater.

Thank you, son, for being my number one fan and supporter. Never give up the pursuit of your dream. You've witnessed the highs and lows of me pushing this book out. Thank God! Thank you for cheering me on. I love you so much.

Thank you, Mom, for your gentle nudging and encouragement; you were always telling me to keep going. I love you to life.

Table of Contents

Foreword xiii
Acknowledgments xv
Introduction xvii
A Note to the Reader xix

Part 1:
Icons and Superheroes - *Know Thyself*

Chapter One: Defining Icons and Superheroes -
What's The Difference? 3
Chapter Two: Batman, Superman, or Wonder Woman -
Who Am I? 7

Part 2:
Legacy or Legend - *Survey of the Land*

Chapter Three: What Size are the Shoes? -
Recognize the Impact of the Previous Individual 13
Chapter Four: Never Belittle Your Predecessor -
Respect is a Springboard to Rapport 17
Chapter Five: Remain Focused -
Distractions Impede Progress 21

Part 3:
You Do You - *No Copycats*

Chapter Six: Creating Your Personal Brand -
Give Them Something to Talk About 31

Part 4:
Laying Your Foundation -
Building Bridges and Forming Alliances

Chapter Seven: Level the Playing Field -
Find Common Interests. 41

Chapter Eight: Say My Name, Say My Name -
Getting on a First Name Basis. 45

Chapter Nine: Keep Your Predecessor on Speed Dial -
Ask for Help 49

Part 5:
"I Brought My Own Shoes" -
Game Plan to Move Forward

Chapter Ten: Be Slow to Change -
Don't Unravel Everything Overnight 53

Chapter Eleven: Never Let Them See You Sweat -
*Handle Problems Efficiently and
Crisis Situations Quickly*. 57

Chapter Twelve: Eye On the Prize -
Immediate Goals; Future Goals 61

Chapter Thirteen: Attitude is Everything -
You Are in Control. 65

Chapter Fourteen: Smile Often, Laugh Out Loud -
Leave a Lasting Impression 73

Resources. 77

About the Author. 79

Foreword

Betty Jewell Slater is a walking, talking, breathing, example of someone who follows in the footsteps of iconic individuals yet brings her own unique style and brand, her shoes, to the role.

I spoke with Betty during a Bay Area Igniting Souls Fellowship and had the pressing urge to invite her to present a monologue at the annual Igniting Souls Conference. During the event, we had the pleasure of meeting Harriet Tubman through her presentation.

The audience was riveted by Betty's ability to transform herself and the room, bringing us alongside Harriet's escape from slavery and rise to prominence as one of the most successful conductors on the Underground Railroad.

Betty decided to co-brand the *Big Shoes to Fill* Message, with the theme in my latest book, *Unhackable*. I am honored. When you're told you have big shoes to fill, seeds of doubt and fear are planted. You may question whether you have what it takes to be successful in the role. You got hacked.

Big Shoes to Fill: How to Establish Your Own Brand When Following In The Footsteps of An Icon, is a timely manual for overcoming the seeds of doubt or fear and for propelling the reader toward new and exciting life roles.

Kary Oberbruner
CEO of Igniting Souls Publishing Agency,
award-winner, author of Elixir Project, Day Job to Dream Job, The Deeper Path, Your Secret Name, and Unhackable

Acknowledgments

When you decide to accomplish something, you can break out on your own, however, it is so much better when you have people in your corner supporting you, pushing you, and reminding you how important it is for you to finish the task.

Writing this book has been a wonderful and challenging journey. I must acknowledge those who heard me speak about the content and then encouraged me along the way. My mom; Betty L. Slater, Pamela Stitt, Charlotte Johnson, Aldane Walters, Qiana Redmond, Rose Pratt-Nervis, and so many others.

Thank you to my beta readers, for your insightful feedback, encouragement, and honesty. I love you Rhonda Roberts and Kerry Ahrend.

Thank you to my book pre-launch party team. I appreciate you Jody Almond, Dr. Yolanda Dawson, my sisters Cynthia Sosa (natural) and Pamela Stitt (sister from another mister), Dawn Baker, and Rhonda Roberts.

Acknowledgments

Everyone needs to be held accountable. Thank you to my Fire Ring and Speaker Academy Elite accountability partners and coach. I appreciate you all so much for cheering me on, for providing a listening ear, and for your valuable feedback: Niccie Kleigel, Doug Fitzgerald, Lisa Thompson Moser, Vivian King, Renee Vidor, Natalie Dawn Hanson, and Martyn Wood.

To my final editor Nanette O'Neal, you are amazing. Thank you for seeing what I didn't see, and for your suggestions that made my thoughts unfold with greater clarity.

Thank you to Kary Oberbruner, David Branderhorst, and the Igniting Souls Tribe. Author Academy Elite is the best for new or previously published authors. The "tribe vibe" is truly fantastic.

Finally, charge it to my head and not my heart those of you who were a part of this journey and I neglected to mention you here. I love you much.

Introduction

It is not only nerve-wracking, but also downright intimidating to step into a role where your predecessor is well-liked, well-known, and well-respected, an icon. Not only are you contending with living up to that individual's legacy in your mind; you are consistently reminded by others that "you have some big shoes to fill," as you attempt to navigate your path in the new role.

Throughout my working career, whenever I took a position where the person I was replacing had left a significant and positive imprint within the department, or upon the organization, inevitably I would be on the receiving end of the phrase, "you've got some big shoes to fill." For years, I would acknowledge indeed I did, until I turned the table and began to say, "Actually, I brought my own shoes."

This was a huge breakthrough. It signified my appreciation and respect for the impact my predecessor had, but it also set me apart. People began to view me in a different light. This new declaration showed I was prepared to meet the standard set by my predecessor, yet I would also work to garner respect for the skills, talent, and ideas I was bringing.

My goal was to exceed the previous standard and establish a new one.

Soon I began to hear the phrase, "you've got some big shoes to fill," about me as I left a position. I met and exceeded the standards of excellence in customer service, I anticipated the needs of the client, solved problems, and contributed to the team. I had become the person well-liked, well-known, and well respected, "the icon".

When reading *Big Shoes To Fill: How To Establish Your Own Brand When Following In The Footsteps Of An Icon*, you will gain the tools needed to effectively brand yourself and leave your mark in your new role.

By using these tips, the intimidation that comes with following in the footsteps of an icon will be lessened, and you will begin to confidently proclaim in response to you've got some big shoes to fill, "Actually, I brought my own shoes!"

A Note to the Reader

Welcome to *Big Shoes to Fill: How to Establish Your Own Brand When Following in The Footsteps of An Icon*. The title is a mouthful within itself, however, you are going to receive an abundance of valuable information to assist you, now and in the future, as you step in and out of new roles. Whatever the role, the information presented here will help you make a successful transition.

The idea for this book came because of my getting laid off from a job I enjoyed. It was a Friday, a few days before my fifth work anniversary and the Thanksgiving holiday. My position had been eliminated; I was let go. My heart raced. I began blinking rapidly to stop the pool of tears blurring my vision. My mind went blank, and all normal comprehension stopped.

Thoughts were coming into my mind at the speed of light. Although I was let go, someone still needed to be onsite to "man the fort," so to speak. Someone needed to be there physically to assist homeowners.

I had been the main point of contact for the last five years. I had developed a special rapport with everyone. I was well-known, well-liked, trusted, and respected—the icon. How would the incoming individual handle the responsibilities of the role?

I worried the individual coming in behind me might be met with suspicion due to the abrupt way I had left. Their ability to do the job would likely come under scrutiny. The level of service homeowners received from the incoming individual might be judged based on the standard they had been accustomed to. They had some "big shoes to fill."

I had personal experience with everything they would encounter. I thought it would be helpful to create a little booklet to help them navigate the work systems I had put in place. It would also provide tips and tools they could use to differentiate themselves from me. This would allow their gifts to move into the spotlight. The information in the booklet would show them how to establish their benchmark for being successful in the role.

Finally, I wanted to encourage the individual not to be intimidated by any of the comparisons that would inevitably come. You are holding the culmination of the notes I wanted to share with that individual, plus some additional valuable information.

Turn the page and embark upon a journey to discover, create, or enhance yourself and your brand.

Once you've completed the book, you will have an increased level of confidence. No one will be able to convince you the shoes of your predecessor are too big to fill. You are unique. No one else can offer what you offer. Get ready to proudly walk in your own shoes!

PART 1

Icons and Superheroes – Know Thyself

CHAPTER ONE

Defining Icons and Superheroes

What's The Difference?

> *"There is a superhero inside all of us;*
> *we just need the courage to put on the cape."*
>
> *~Anonymous*

It is important to recognize whom you are dealing with or the magnitude of the impact your predecessor has had in the role you are stepping into. Several questions to consider are:

- Is your predecessor an icon or a superhero?
- Is there a difference?
- Does it matter?

What comes to mind when you hear the word icon? What about a superhero? Your predecessor may fall into one or both of these categories. If you are clear about the definitions of these words, you will have the first key toward "bringing your own shoes" to your new role.

Icon:

The online dictionary; https://www.yourdictionary.com defines the word icon as:

1. Any person or thing that is revered; one who is the object of great attention and devotion, or idol.
2. Something regarded as embodying the essential characters of an era or group etc.
3. A person or thing that is the best example of a certain profession or some doing.

The https://www.merriam-webster.com online dictionary defines an icon as - An object of uncritical devotion

Superhero:

To remain consistent with the source of the definitions, https://www.yourdictionary.com was used to define superhero as:

1. A made-up character having superpowers and abilities.
2. Any person regarded as having extraordinary ability in some field.
3. A heroic fictional character, of a kind found in comic books, who has physical and mental abilities, skills, etc. that are superhuman or superior to those of an ordinary human being.

The https://www.yourdictionary.com online dictionary defines a superhero as an exceptionally skillful or successful person.

Now that the words icon and superhero have been defined, it is important to consider the following ideas as you determine where your predecessor lies concerning our earlier questions. Is your predecessor an icon or a superhero? Is there a difference? Does it matter?

- The icon and the superhero may be ordinary human beings' *other* human beings have elevated to a status of such proportion almost anyone would be intimidated when following in their footsteps.
- Both icons and superheroes may be regarded as those with exceptional success, skill, or abilities.
- An icon and a superhero may be the same person.
- Pop culture and the entertainment industry thrive on the establishment of icons and superheroes.
- It is hard to live up to a made-up character.
- Increase your awareness of up-and-coming icons and superheroes; and what makes them such.

Some people work or train diligently to attain certain levels of proficiency in their field. The only limitations to an individual becoming top-notch, an ace, or number one are those they place upon themselves. The true icon and superhero is the individual who never stops moving in the direction of their goals no matter what challenges (physical, mental, or otherwise) come their way.

There is no difference between the title's icon and superhero when referring to your predecessor, therefore, it doesn't matter which title they have been given, both are lauded upon the individual who has put in the time to become the best at what they do.

In chapter two, we will examine how you see yourself. Your self-image and your self-talk contribute to any limiting beliefs that keep you from bringing your shoes to your new role. See you in the next chapter!

CHAPTER TWO

Batman, Superman, or Wonder Woman

Who Am I?

"A hero can be anyone. Even a man doing something as simple as putting a coat around a little boy's shoulders to let him know the world hadn't ended."

~Anonymous

Superheroes have unique supernatural strengths, abilities, or skills. None of them have the same ability. They are a force to be reckoned with individually, and when they work together, their strengths are enhanced.

Let's take a look at Batman, Superman, and Wonder Woman.

Batman - Batman does not possess superpowers, per se. He relies on his genius intellect, physical prowess, martial arts abilities, detective skills, science and technology, vast wealth, intimidation, and indomitable will. (Wiki)

Superman - Superman does possess superpowers. He has super strength, he flies, he has x-ray vision, invulnerability, speed, heat vision, freezing breath, superflare (a recently added massive, omnidirectional heat blast that obliterates anything within a quarter-mile radius), and superhuman senses. Superman can travel at the speed of light. (Wiki)

Wonder Woman - Wonder Woman's Amazonian training helped her develop a wide range of extraordinary skills in tactics, hunting, and combat. She possesses an arsenal of advanced technology including the Lasso of Truth, a pair of indestructible bracelets, a tiara that serves as a projectile, and, in older stories, a range of devices based on Amazon technology.

Just as these characters have unique abilities to draw from at a moment's notice, you have unique gifts, talents, and skills, also known as your superpowers, to draw upon. They allow you to spring into action and provide stable leadership.

It doesn't matter whether you have been in the game one day or one hundred days, your skills are valuable and are needed in your new role.

Take inventory of yourself. What are your superpowers (your skills, talents, and abilities)? What do you do exceptionally well? List them below. Ask a trusted friend or family member for help with this exercise to remind you of some of your strengths.

1. _____ 3. _____
2. _____ 4. _____

5. _____ 8. _____
6. _____ 9. _____
7. _____ 10._____

If you run out of room, get an additional sheet of paper, and keep going. Once finished, give yourself kudos. Save your answers. You will need them in chapter six.

These are the essential elements of your personal brand. You may have discovered skills that were dormant. This list proves you have exactly what it takes to be successful. You are the superhero for your new role, the icon. Read on to discover the size of your predecessors' shoes and assess what you are up against.

PART 2

Legacy or Legend – Survey of the Land

CHAPTER THREE

What Size are the Shoes?

Recognize the Impact of the Previous Individual

"I've got big shoes to fill. This is my chance to do something. I have to seize the moment."
~Andrew Jackson

When you step into a new role, the worst thing you can do is compare yourself to your predecessor. Everyone else is already making comparisons, so you should stay out of it. Superherocs don't compare themselves to one another they simply use their individual skills when needed.

You don't want to compare yourself, but you may want to assess the skills your predecessor brought to the role and learn what made them successful. Your task is to discover how they became the icon.

Take an inventory of their skills to determine whether any of them may be of use to you. Consider how the individual used the skills that contributed to their success. If a skill positively impacted their role and it is one you also possess, place it in your quiver to be used at the appropriate time. If it is not a skill you possess, take note of it for possible future reference. If it didn't contribute to their success, don't give it a second thought.

How do you assess the skills someone else has? Use the tactics of observation and interaction. To observe is to watch the individual in action. To interact is to engage with them one-on-one or in a group.

During your training, pay attention, be direct, and ask a lot of questions. Example: "What contributed to your success in this role?" It is amazing how many people are willing to share their success strategies.

Typically, I would hear the statement, "You've got big shoes to fill," while I was being trained by my predecessor. I simply smiled and nodded in agreement.

If you don't have the luxury of learning from your predecessor before stepping into your new role, don't panic. Use your exemplary communication skills (surely you listed that as one of your superpowers) to gather the information you need.

Another strategy for discovering another's skills and for learning how to incorporate those skills into your role is to listen to the office chatter. You can learn a lot by listening to others as they reminisce about the "good times" they experienced with a colleague who has moved on.

Before you use this tactic, be sure to have a solid personal boundary established. You are not using this strategy to gossip. Your goal is to gain an understanding of your predecessor's impact. Remove yourself from the conversation if it becomes a gossip session. Proactively encourage conversations that highlight the things that worked and those that didn't. Be intentional about getting details that highlight best practices.

When I genuinely showed interest in how things worked previously, I was able to quiet some of the fear people had about whether I was going to come in and change everything. Although some change was needed and necessary, (we'll discuss this in chapter ten), the changes weren't going to be immediate, nor without an understanding of current processes and systems.

Your objective is to gain a clear picture of the impact the previous individual had. You need to know the size of the proverbial shoes to be filled. With this knowledge, you can begin making plans for your success in the role.

CHAPTER FOUR

Never Belittle Your Predecessor

Respect is a Springboard to Rapport

> *"You never look good trying to make someone else look bad."*
>
> ~ Unknown

Success in your new role will depend partially on developing rapport with the individuals loyal to your predecessor. Building rapport is gaining the respect and mutual trust of others. Rapport can happen quickly when you meet someone new, or it may take some time to develop.

Finding common interests is necessary when developing rapport (we will delve into common interests in chapter seven).

Make your predecessor the springboard to developing rapport with the team. Look for opportunities to genuinely praise their work and accomplishments during their tenure. This sends the message you can be trusted (developing rapport requires trust). You can't be that bad if you have positive things to say about someone they highly respect.

There are specific actions you can take to be intentional about building rapport. Don't be swept up with office gossip or politics, and never, ever, speak negatively of the individual who was in the position previously. You will experience an immediate loss of credibility if you engage in such behavior.

An article on the MindTools career website; Building Rapport, Establishing Strong Two-Way Connections describes three elements present when rapport has been established:

Mutual attentiveness - which is being focused on and interested in what the other person says or does.

Positivity — the individuals are friendly, happy, and show care and concern for each other.

Coordination — the feeling of being "in sync." The body language and energy of individuals appear to be like each other.

The article goes on to state that having rapport gives you the influence to learn and teach. Be mindful of this; rapport isn't simply about relationship building, it is the foundation for success.

How do you build rapport?

The following steps are basic to building rapport.

"Fix your face." A friend of mine would say this when my facial expressions were less than complimentary. In other words, smile, don't frown. Since you won't have a second chance to make a good first impression, smile when you meet people. A frown causes individuals to be more guarded when they meet you, especially the first time. A smile is welcoming and it invites connection.

Look for common interests. When you have something in common with another person, you begin developing a relationship organically. Be sincere when communicating about the shared interest(s) you have.

Show concern for others. Theodore Roosevelt once said, "People don't care how much you know until they know how much you care." Showing genuine concern for others is a barrier breaker.

Be friendly towards everyone. A quote from an ancient book of wisdom, The Bible says, "He who has friends must first show himself friendly." Proverbs 18:24 (KJV) - Let friendliness be your reputation and your key to unlocking the door to rapport.

Now, that rapport has been established, let's get focused, and set some goals.

CHAPTER FIVE

Remain Focused

Distractions Impede Progress

"Focus on your goal. Don't look in any direction but ahead."

~Anonymous

It is easy to become distracted by the foray caused by your appearance on the scene. It may not matter whether your role comes through a promotion or as a brand-new face within the organization. Decide in advance not to allow the attitudes of others (positive or negative) to deter you from being successful. You want to leave your mark on the organizational culture. If we want to leave a legacy within our personal and professional lives, eliminating distractions is a must.

Don't allow the statement, "you have big shoes to fill," to intimidate or keep you from being focused and taking the necessary steps to become successful.

One success step is to keep your focus. This may be easier said than done. According to Brett and Kate McKay, authors of a two-part series called *What Every Man Should Know about Focus*, "People really want to master their attention, but they don't know what attention is."

What comes to mind when you hear the word focus or the word attention? In the article, the McKays define attention as, "the ability to focus on certain stimuli or thoughts while ignoring others, which shapes how we perceive and experience the world around us."

The definition of focus according to webster.com is to concentrate attention or effort. Focus requires us to pay attention. In your new role, your focus should not be directed toward your predecessor.

Many things will vie for your attention; it is important to know how to set priorities. As you become inundated with meetings, deadlines, and emergencies, managing your focus is paramount.

How do you prioritize? What do you do when everything screams to become a priority? According to the article *Focus: The Ultimate Guide on How to Improve Focus and Concentration* by James Clear, "Focus is the key to productivity because saying no to every other option unlocks your ability to accomplish the one thing that is left."

With that in mind, the task now is to figure out what to focus on. Let's take a look at two strategies for maintaining focus. There are many strategies available, however, I found these easy to implement right away.

Warren Buffett's "2 List" Strategy for Focused Attention

The first strategy, which is found in James Clear's article shares the method billionaire Warren Buffett uses for focused attention. In my opinion, if Warren Buffet uses this technique, it's worth putting it to the test for ourselves.

Step One: Write down the top 25 career goals you have.

You may adjust the list based on your needs. You might have a project-specific due date. If that is the case, list all the tasks associated with completing the project by the set deadline, and then follow the subsequent steps. Another way to use the list as mentioned in the article is to list the top 25 tasks you want to accomplish during the upcoming week. Rather than career goals, you may want to use them for your personal or business goals. The decision is yours.

1. _____
2. _____
3. _____
4. _____
5. _____
6. _____
7. _____
8. _____
9. _____
10. _____
11. _____
12. _____
13. _____
14. _____
15. _____
16. _____
17. _____
18. _____
19. _____
20. _____
21. _____
22. _____
23. _____
24. _____
25. _____

Step Two: Review the list and only circle the top five goals.

It might be agonizing, but you may only choose the five most important items. Once you've made your choices, you will focus your attention on the five items circled. Are you ready for step three? Let's go.

Step Three: The items you didn't circle belong to your AVOID AT ALL COST LIST.

This list receives no attention whatsoever until you have completed all five items you circled. What just happened? You identified the focus thieves. The goals you didn't circle are tasks that don't make the best use of your time. They are the distractions that keep you from narrowing your focus and reaching your goals.

A big plus is the adrenaline rush and sense of accomplishment you receive for checking a goal off the list.

I find this technique very helpful when I have several projects, I'm responsible for at the same time or when I need a to-do list on a particular day. I list everything that needs to be accomplished regardless of the project. I circle the top five goals. I then prioritize the top five and begin working.

A big plus is the adrenaline rush and sense of accomplishment you receive for checking a goal off the list. True to the strategy, I don't look at anything else until the top five are finished. IMPORTANT: Don't allow email to interrupt your focus. Certainly, you may need to respond to an urgent email or an email with information relevant to the task. After you respond, quickly get back on track.

Mayo Oshin is a researcher who writes about ideas for better productivity, creativity, and decision-making. His article, The Ivy Lee Method: A 100-year-old, 15-Minute Routine for Stress-Free Productivity, describes a system to help you focus your attention and become more productive in all areas of your life. The system is as practical today as when it was first introduced.

The Ivy Lee Method

In the 1900s, Charles Schwab wanted to increase productivity within the executive team at the Bethlehem Steel Corporation of which Schwab was president. He was directed to Ivy Lee, a respected productivity expert. After listening to Schwab, Lee requested fifteen minutes with each of the company executives.

Lee offered his services free of charge if his method did not work. After ninety days, Schwab was to write Lee a check for whatever he felt it was worth if the method was successful. At the end of the ninety days, Schwab wrote Lee a check for $25,000.00 (the equivalent of $400,000.00 in 2018). Wow! Show me the money. What did Lee talk about during his fifteen minutes with each executive? It is the process called the Ivy Lee Method.

The Process:

Define your vision, goals, and objectives for each area of your life (relationships, business, health, finances, and spirit).

Every night, list the six most important things you want to accomplish the next day (don't list more than six items). Prioritize the list with the most important task first and the least important one last.

Each day, begin working on the most important task and work down the list. Don't move to the next task until the previous one has been completed.

At the end of the day, if there are any remaining tasks on the list, move them to the list for the next day.

Repeat this process daily.

These steps require fifteen minutes of your time each night in exchange for a lifetime of increased focus. You will achieve your goals, and you will see improvement in your productivity levels, health, and relationships.

There are some similarities between the Warren Buffet Method and the Ivy Lee Method. They are simple enough to begin using immediately. Trying to implement a complex system can be perceived as a barrier to getting focused. If a process is too complicated, it is less likely to be maintained or even begun. Both systems provide a method for being consistent which is a key element in maintaining focus.

When using any system for maintaining focus, make sure to build in periodic breaks. No matter how great a system is, no one can maintain consistent focus without their concentration waning. Along with planned breaks, include a metric for measuring your progress. James Clear says, "It is only through numbers and clear tracking that we have any idea if we are getting better or worse."

His article notes that measuring isn't about judging your progress; rather, it is an aide to maintaining your focus long-term.

Try both systems, and then share your experience with me. There is information in the back of the book on how to connect with me online to share.

Now, let's use your focus to create or strengthen your brand.

PART 3

You Do You – No Copycats

CHAPTER SIX

Creating Your Personal Brand
Give Them Something to Talk About

> *"Don't be scared to present the real you to the world; authenticity is at the heart of success."*
>
> *– unknown*

Developing your personal brand is your best strategy for stepping out of your predecessor's shadow. Whether you are aware of it or not, "you" are a brand. Let's take the time right now to determine whether your brand is being created organically (it is being formed with no specific direction or plan), whether you have made a conscious effort to shape it (you are putting in the work to define it), or whether it needs to be scrapped altogether and undergo a full makeover (it is a toss-up between organic creation and a few attempts by you or someone you know, to define it).

What is a personal brand? According to Tom Peters, the man credited with introducing the concept of personal branding, the job of marketing ourselves as the CEO of ME Inc. is the crux of what personal branding is all about. He says, "Our most important job is to be head marketer of the brand called you."

A Forbes magazine article by Homaira Kabir also addresses the concept of personal branding. Kabir says, "The core of personal branding is giving people the words to talk about you when you're not around. It's about letting others know how you can be of service."

Kabir's quote establishes the need for you to be in control of your brand. You can allow your brand's message to be generated organically where you have no control over the words being formulated to describe you and your services, or you can become the head marketer of your brand as Tom Peters suggests, and make the determination about which words will be used to discuss you. No one will be more competent than you, at describing who you are in the most favorable way possible. If you allow your brand words to form organically, the outcome is likely to be significantly different than what you would have expected or wanted.

Creating your personal brand requires taking specific action. There are many articles and blogs describing how to create your brand. We will be using steps found in Forbes.

One of the key points to remember regarding personal branding is the fact that your brand is who you are all the time, whether in a work or social environment. Knowing who you are and what you have to offer the world should be clear if you desire to convey your message consistently.
How do you create your brand?

The following steps will assist you in creating a strong personal brand.

1. Figure out who you are

In chapter two, you wrote down at least ten of your superpowers or skills. Expand that list by adding words to describe your strengths, values, beliefs, and the things you are passionate about. These words form the nucleus of who you are as an individual.

You were also supposed to ask a trusted friend or family member to help you identify your skills. Do it again, but this time, ask them to share the words that pop up in their mind when they think about you. Be prepared for some unexpected revelations about how you are perceived. If any of the feedback is negative, don't take it personally. Use the negative feedback to reflect. Is there some truth to what is being said? If so, determine what needs to change. If you can't see what they are highlighting, don't agonize over it. Pin it for review at another time. Creating your brand begins with getting an understanding of who you are.

2. Decide what you want to be known for.

Assess what you bring to the table. Your personal brand should reflect your skills, values, passions, and beliefs.

Take the list you created in chapter two and categorize all the words into one of the columns below (use a separate sheet of paper if necessary).

Skills/Strengths	Values	Passions	Beliefs

Once all the words are listed, look at your skills and determine the area in which you want to become recognized as the authority. You may have more than one area where you can be an authority, but for now, choose only one. It could be the area you are currently working in, or you may find your passion is in a totally different area. This exercise is to reveal what you want to be known for and build your brand accordingly.

3. Determine your target audience.

The quote, "A jack of all trades is a master of none, but oftentimes better than a master of one," by Elizabethan English, is used about a person who has dabbled in many skills rather than gaining expertise by focusing on one.

The shortened version, "a jack of all trades," is often a compliment for a person who is good at fixing things and has a broad knowledge of how things work. This individual knows enough from many learned trades and skills to be able to bring the individual disciplines all together in a practical way. This person is a generalist rather than a specialist. When it comes to the task you want to be known for, you want to be the specialist.

4. Write your value proposition statement.

What is a value proposition statement and why do you need one? To build your personal brand, it is important for your customer to know who you are (what you're known for), what you do (your product or service), and how you can help them (their pain point).

If no one knows what you do, they can't purchase your product. People purchase products from individuals they trust, but if they don't know you, they can't trust you. Their pain point is eased by your competitor.

The value proposition statement fills the role of informing your customer that your product or service is exactly what they need. In one sentence they find out who you are, what you do, and how you can help them.

The format I used to write my value proposition statement comes from my business mentor who is an author, publisher, and leader of the Igniting Souls Tribe, Kary Oberbrunner.

I am a _____, who helps _____, do/understand _____, so that _____.

Betty's value proposition statement:

"I am a film and stage producer, a coach, actor, speaker, and author, who helps individuals, organizations, and actors identify and break through limiting systems, ideas, and beliefs so that they can experience unhackability, be all they were created to be, and impact the Kingdom of God in their niche, all over the world."

The next time someone asks about what you do for a living, your value proposition statement summarizes it succinctly for you. I encourage you to memorize it and embrace it!

The next four steps for creating your personal brand, center around communicating your brand message with actions that reflect the words you used to describe your skills, strengths, values, passions, and beliefs. The words you in step two are the foundation of who you are, and who you are, is revealed in what you do. Let's continue.

5. Tell your story.

Your personal brand is about communicating your story to your target audience in a way they can engage with and relate to. Did you overcome some obstacles blocking your success? Did you keep striving for a particular goal during all kinds of adversity? Knowing that you, too, have experienced difficult times and overcome them may help your audience see you as authentic.

Your story is also connected to your value proposition statement. It fills in the blanks surrounding how you arrived on the scene. This is helpful when stepping into a new role, as questions about your background may be answered. When you share your story, it is helpful to use examples your audience understands or is familiar with.

6. Be consistent.

In step two of the brand process, you are clarifying the one thing you want to be known for. Once you are recognized as the authority for a particular area, you may then expand your reach by incorporating another area into your brand message. If you communicate more than one message in the early stages of building your brand, your audience will become confused and possibly move on to follow someone with a more clear and more consistent message. Consistency with your message extends to your social media platforms and your website if you have an online presence.

7. Live your brand.

Your personal brand is not a separate entity that can be picked up, put down, put on, or put off based on your circumstances or the surroundings you find yourself in. You are your brand; you live it every day. Make sure you are representing yourself well.

Tim Salau, community builder and founder of the organization Mentors & Mentees, who works with college students to help them build brands that will get them hired says, "Your personal brand should follow you everywhere you go. It needs to be an authentic manifestation of who you are and amplify what you believe."

You are your brand; you live it every day. Make sure you are representing yourself well.

Each previous step in the brand-building process provides the foundation for the next one, so when you arrive here at step seven, all the steps in the process culminate into a concise effort to present the intentionally created brand called you to the world.

As you continue building your brand, pay attention to inconsistencies between your brand message and your actions; keep your brand in alignment.

Here is a recap of the personal branding steps. Tom Peterson said, "Our most important job is to be head marketer of the brand called you." You may want to return to these steps time and again to assure your personal brand is a clear indication of your growth, and any new skills you gain.

Review the questions below to highlight the steps for creating your personal brand.

1. Do you know who you are?
2. What are you known for now? What do you want to be known for?
3. Who is your target audience?
4. What is your value proposition statement?
5. Can you articulate the story surrounding your brand?
6. Is your brand message consistent?
7. Are you living your brand?

Your personal brand is intact. In chapter seven we will form alliances through common interests.

PART 4

Laying Your Foundation – Building Bridges and Forming Alliances

CHAPTER SEVEN

Level the Playing Field

Find Common Interests

"Shared values and common interests—much more can be built on these than on gratitude alone."
~Horst Koehler

Chapter four discussed how to build rapport. Finding common interests was mentioned as a step in developing rapport. Let's explore this further.

Common Interest is sharing an interest in an activity such as traveling or a hobby like painting or sharing a particular community or world view regarding an issue like healthcare.

Having common interests with others helps level the playing field in your new role. You've entered the scene on the heels of someone well-liked, well-loved, and well-respected. It is important to differentiate yourself from that individual. Initially, you may feel overshadowed by their reputation. When you build rapport within the organization, it provides a foundation for establishing your brand of leadership.

How exactly do you go about finding common interests with someone?

Smile. A smile helps remove barriers of distrust as you begin reaching out to people. Smiles create a welcoming, caring, atmosphere. Showing care opens people up to you. A quote by the author of the best-selling audio series, *The Art of Winning* Denis Waitley says, "A smile is the light in your window that tells others that there is a caring, sharing person inside." Don't pretend to have interest in someone; be interested in who they are.

Ask questions. Use open-ended questions to discover common interests. You may discover shared values. People have come to realize they have mutual acquaintances, or they enjoy the same author. Open-ended questions are an excellent way to become aware of the similarities you share with someone.

Listen actively. People love to talk about themselves, their families, and their hobbies or interests. Active listening helps you ask meaningful questions which also allows you to discover common interests. How do you actively listen? Steven Covey says, "Seek to understand." So, listen to "understand" what is being shared, not simply to hear it. The following steps highlight the practice of active listening.

1. Pay Attention
2. Show That You're Listening

3. Provide Feedback
4. Defer Judgement

Respond appropriately. I can't stress enough the importance of being genuine in your interactions. People recognize fake interest. If you are not genuine, the process of building rapport will be stagnated, if not halted altogether. You don't know how much time you'll lose nor how long it will take to regain enough trust to begin the process again.

Discovering a common interest with another individual isn't rocket science. It's as simple as enjoying a particular genre of music, discussing the best lines from certain movies, or sharing travel hacks.

When you use common interests to build rapport, you continue the process of establishing yourself in your role and building your personal brand.

Once you discover common interests with individuals, the natural progression in the relationship is to advance from formal titles, if they exist, to a first-name basis. In chapter eight, we will discuss the importance of names.

CHAPTER EIGHT

Say My Name, Say My Name
Getting on a First Name Basis

"There is no sound so sweet as the sound of one's own name."
- William Shakespeare

A person's name is the first official label they receive in life. It is their identifier. It can be a label that instills a sense of pride within the individual, or it can be a label of constant humiliation and embarrassment when the name is mispronounced or changed without the individual's permission to accommodate the person pronouncing it.

Today, the U.S. business culture is less formal; people tend to get on a first-name basis almost immediately. In other cultures, there is still a more formal approach to names in the business. A good book to learn about other business customs is *Kiss, Bow, or Shake Hands: How to do Business in 60 Different Countries* by Terri Morrison and Wayne Conaway.

It is a critical component of your success in your new role to remember people's names. Remembering people's names speaks volumes about your commitment to building rapport with them.

It is as equally important to pronounce their name correctly. This also communicates they matter to you. We live in a global society which allows us to appreciate people of all cultures, many of whom have names that are difficult to pronounce. If it is a particularly difficult name, make an effort to learn how to pronounce it properly. Take the time to learn it. Pronouncing it correctly honors who they are. Their respect for you increases, and they become more comfortable working with you. You'll initiate a new level of influence with that individual.

Names have significance and meaning. In some cultures, the naming of a child is a ceremonial or celebratory event. The naming of an individual in such a manner essentially establishes their identity and significance within the culture. When I contemplated names for my son, I wanted a name that would pay tribute to his father yet command respect before he ever stepped foot into the room. I didn't allow anyone to shorten his name or give him a nickname until he was at an age to determine for himself what that would be. There was no formal ceremony, but that didn't matter—the choosing of his name held the same significance.

Resist the tendency to brush over a difficult name to pronounce, shorten a long name, or give someone a nickname without their permission.

I'm reminded of a time I was sitting in a social service office waiting for my name to be called by a counselor. I was unemployed, but in school full-time. I had made an appointment to request assistance. Once you registered at the intake counter, you were to wait for a counselor to call your name. The room was crowded, and a counselor stepped in to call out a name. She did so several times, however, no one came forward. It was evident the name was a difficult one to pronounce. The individual being called did not realize they were being summoned because they didn't hear their name as it should be pronounced.

A person's name is music to their ears. By taking time to remember and correctly pronounce names, you put yourself in a position to win over those who may have been on the fence about you.

What can you do to become proficient at remembering and pronouncing names correctly?

These tips should help.

- When you meet someone for the first time, pay close attention to how they say their name, and pronounce their name out loud immediately after they say it.
- Don't be afraid to ask someone to repeat their name if you missed it or didn't understand them. They may be flattered you took the time to ask.
- During the course of the conversation, repeat someone's name a minimum of three times to seal it in your memory.
- Associate the name with a catchy phrase, an animal, or anything else that will help you remember it.

Do whatever it takes to master remembering and pronouncing names. The quote by William Shakespeare at the beginning of this chapter sums it up perfectly. "There is no sound so sweet as the sound of one's own name."

One of the best things you can do to remember names is to be intentional. Make it a priority. Your name will be remembered, revered, and respected as a result.

CHAPTER NINE

Keep Your Predecessor on Speed Dial

Ask for Help

"Having someone help you doesn't mean you failed.
It just means you're not in it alone."

~Anonymous

You are smart, confident, and experienced. At some point, however, you may need help in your new role. The worst thing you can do to yourself is to pretend you have it all together, when, you simply need a little nudge in the proper direction.

Asking for help is a sign of wisdom and strength, not weakness. Be willing to ask for help early because that's when you are operating on a learning curve, and the grace to receive the help you need is high. Take advantage during these early stages to explore the depth of your role, make assessments about the direction you want to take, and consider your long-term goals.

Make the following lyrics "I ain't 2 proud, I ain't 2 proud 2 beg" from the song *Ain't 2 Proud 2 Beg* by the group, TLC your anthem. This is not to imply asking for help is begging. It is to impress upon you not to let pride stop you from getting the help you need.

The best time to ask for help is:

- After you've exhausted all options to solve an issue on your own.
- When not asking for help means wasted time.
- If there will be a project delay.
- When stalling makes you appear incompetent.
- When you feel like you should be able to handle things, yet you're exasperated.

Whom should you ask?

If you received training from your predecessor, get permission to contact them if you get in a tight situation. If you don't have access to the individual who held the position previously, consider your direct supervisor.

Before you reach out to anyone, especially your predecessor, take a moment to gather other questions or concerns that have surfaced. You'll want to make the most productive use of the time to cover your concerns and anything else that will help you be successful.

Give yourself permission to seek help when necessary, and let's move forward.

PART 5

"I Brought My Own Shoes" - Game Plan to Move Forward

CHAPTER TEN

Be Slow to Change

Don't Unravel Everything Overnight

> *"Work for a cause, not for applause, live life to express, not to impress. Don't strive to make your presence noticed, just make your absence felt."*
>
> *- Unknown*

One area in life where there is usually great resistance is regarding the change. Although change is necessary for growth, the natural inclination for most people is to avoid it at all costs rather than embrace it.

A great book to read about embracing change is *Who Moved My Cheese?* by Spencer Johnson. It is a parable about two mice, (Sniff and Scurry) and two men, (Hem and Haw) who gather cheese from the same location for years. One day, they arrive to find the cheese has vanished. It is not in its normal, familiar spot. They all have a decision to make concerning this change. Will they embrace the change and seek a new source for cheese, or will they stubbornly expect the cheese to reappear as suddenly as it disappeared?

As you become acclimated to your new role and its responsibilities, you may be able to change systems and processes which you determine to have outlived their usefulness. Use wisdom; resist the urge to make major changes right away. Instead, make calculated changes over some time based on your observation of the current internal culture and the systems already at work.

The article, "How to Be Manager to Your Friends and Peers," by Jeremy Anderberg cautions readers to take time to get used to their position before making big changes. By doing so, he says, "You won't appear impulsive." Giving yourself time allows the changes you implement to come across as well-planned and measured which, in turn, gains you the respect of the team.

At times, making an immediate change is necessary and unavoidable. If this is the case, clearly communicating the need (the why) for the change is a must.

In a Forbes Under 30 Network article, one of the four things columnist Samuel Edwards suggests when someone receives their first promotion is to "begin looking for quick and meaningful wins by discovering pain points with team members and searching out ways to address them." This allows you to make smaller changes that give you momentum in your position. The team will begin to rally behind you." This is sound advice for those over thirty as well.

Chapter Ten: Be Slow to Change

The need for change in your new role is inevitable, and how you manage to implement the necessary changes is critical to establishing your legacy. Make it part of your overall strategy to make changes gradually. You will be well-respected for it.

CHAPTER ELEVEN

Never Let Them See You Sweat

Handle Problems Efficiently and Crisis Situations Quickly

> *"To be the best, you must be able to handle the worst."*
> *-Anonymous*

In a perfect world, there would never be challenges, problems, or crises. Everything would always work out the way it is supposed to, no one would ever be late, and every meeting would start on time. Since we don't live in that world, you must be prepared to handle problems or manage crises when they arise.

During many job interviews, you are asked to describe how you've previously handled a difficult situation and to describe the steps you took to manage a crisis. The answers to these questions provide insight into how you might handle challenges that arise in your new role.

Most problems might not reach crisis level if they are handled quickly and efficiently at the beginning. There is no guarantee, however, that a given situation won't escalate straight to a crisis without warning. Here is a review of the skills you need during a crisis.

Communication Skills. To handle problems efficiently, the ability to communicate details of the situation concisely across all levels of the organization is important.

Problem Solving Skills. It is essential to have the ability to solve problems by using strategic and creative thinking to provide possible solutions to the issue at hand.

Analytical Skills. The ability to analyze all aspects of a problem and quickly determine the root cause, not just the symptoms when assessing how to resolve it will play a key role in your distinguishing yourself as a valuable resource for your organization.

The Ability to Remain Calm. Remaining calm during a crisis provides the energy required to use the other skills involved in handling the problem. Your calm demeanor will be a source of strength others can draw from.

While possessing these skills is important, keep in mind some organizations may already have systems in place to handle crisis situations. Request the manual, checklist, or pamphlet detailing these systems and become familiar with the protocols long before a situation presents itself.

The way you handle problems will either strengthen or weaken your brand and reputation. Proficiency in the skills mentioned puts you in a position of strength when managing a crisis. Leading from a position of strength is typically a boost to anyone's reputation.

CHAPTER TWELVE

Eye On the Prize

Immediate Goals; Future Goals

> *"Happy are those who dream dreams and are willing to pay the price to make them come true."*
>
> *~Anonymous*

Setting goals is a non-negotiable task if you are serious about achieving success in your new role and leaving your mark on the organization. Goals are the foundational aspect of any life strategy whether in relationships, finances, health, or business. Benjamin Franklin is credited with the quote, "If you fail to plan; then you plan to fail." Setting goals is the equivalent of planning for a successful tenure in your role.

Sharlyn Lauby writes in the blog article, *3 Types of Goals You Should Set This Year*, about the types of goals you should set. They are time-based, focus-based, and topic-based.

Time-Based. Setting time-based goals is where the phrases short-term, medium-term, and long-term come from regarding goal setting. Time-based goals are set based on achieving them within a certain time frame.

Focus Based. In focused goals, your time, attention, and energy are targeted to completing a singular project. The project is the focus.

Topic-Based. Topic-based goals refer to a specific aspect of our lives such as the desire to learn a new language or to complete a particular degree program.

In the post, Lauby went on to describe the difference between goals and objectives.

A goal is described as a task you want to accomplish, for example, losing weight. Objectives are described as the steps or specific actions required to reach the goal. When you set goals, it is important you pick goals that make sense for what you want to achieve. Your goals must be relevant.

One well-known system for setting relevant goals is the S.M.A.R.T. plan. The acrostic stands for Specific, Measurable, Achievable or (Actionable), Realistic, and Time-bound.

Specific. Know exactly what it is you want to accomplish. Being vague won't help you.

Measurable. How will you know you've reached the goal? Being measurable outlines the completed tasks.

Achievable. Specify the steps or actions (the objectives) you must take to reach the goal.

Realistic. A realistic goal must work with your psychology. You must believe you can and will reach the goal. If subconsciously, you don't believe you can reach the goal, you've already positioned yourself for failure. If it is realistic, it is attainable, but you must seriously evaluate the plausibility of your goals and be truthful with yourself about attaining them. For example, it's not a realistic goal for a 57-year-old-woman to become a professional basketball player in a year if she never played before in her life. This doesn't mean she's a failure; it means the goal was not realistic.

Time-bound. There must be a set completion date. No date or a rolling date confirms you likely won't reach your goal. A deadline focuses your attention on taking the steps toward reaching the goal.

Consider goals as the compass for your life. A compass is a navigational tool. Goals help you navigate towards optimal success and achievement in every area. Begin your success journey by setting three, six, nine, and twelve-month goals. These are time-based as described in the Sharlyn Lauby article. Next, use the S.M.A.R.T. method to break down the strategy needed for completing the goals.

At the end of each quarter, examine your progress and then make the necessary adjustments in your strategy to assure the achievement of the goals. By the end of the year, you will have an outline detailing your advancement in the new role. Making the necessary adjustments along the way may motivate you to reach higher and set bigger goals going forward.

Setting and attaining your goals is important, yet it is even more important to take note of the person you're becoming through achieving the goal. Henry David Thoreau said, "What you get by achieving your goals is not as important as what you become by achieving your goals."

Success in setting and achieving your goals may assist with establishing the legacy you want to leave within the organization.

CHAPTER THIRTEEN

Attitude is Everything
You Are in Control

"For success, attitude is equally as important as ability."
~Anonymous

You can change every aspect of your life if you change your attitude about it.

Whether you have a positive or negative attitude, the challenging situations in your life will be influenced by it and either become unsurmountable or the catalyst for you to have great breakthroughs. Any obstacle can be turned into an advantage when you have the right attitude.

What is the definition of attitude? According to www.dictionary.com, attitude is a manner of acting, feeling, or thinking that shows one's disposition, opinion, etc. Your attitude is like a magnet. A negative attitude draws negative responses to you, and a positive attitude draws positive responses.

The attitude you bring to your new role will influence the team, the goals you want to accomplish, and your future within the organization. Your predecessor left an indelible imprint within the organization, however, your attitude as you take on the role lays the groundwork for leaving your imprint. You will leave a lasting impression for someone to follow as well. The concept of leaving a lasting impression is discussed in chapter fourteen.

You alone are in control of your attitude. No one else can determine what it will be. There is a quote by Zig Ziglar that says, "Attitude, not aptitude, determines your altitude." In other words, your attitude directly correlates to the level of success you achieve. The most successful individuals usually have a great attitude.

New endeavors come with new challenges. As you settle into your role, it is in your best interest to maintain a good attitude.

What are some ways to enhance our attitude?

Stay Positive. Decide to keep a positive outlook no matter what the circumstances are. You can't control what happens to you. You can, however, control your attitude about what happens to you. Whether you're determined to be positive or to be negative, the choice is yours. Keeping a positive attitude may be easy for some people but not for everyone. It takes a conscious effort and a lot of focus to maintain a positive outlook.

Never Compare Yourself to Others. Never compare yourself to anyone else. The number one selling book of all time, The Bible, has the following statement which relates to who you are. You are fearfully and wonderfully made in the image of God. Psalm 139:14; Genesis 1:27 (KJV). You can't get any better than that. It is a grave mistake to compare yourself to others. Comparison is the killer of your individuality and creativity.

There is only one person who has the unique talents you were born with and the skills you've gained along your life's journey. Take what you have, use it to its fullest potential in your new role, and help as many people as you can while you're at it.

Be Confident. The more positive things you incorporate into your life, the more you cultivate confidence. A positive attitude can help build your confidence. The more positive you are, the more confident you become.

Fear can rob you of confidence. Confidence isn't the lack of fear; it is doing what needs to be done despite your fear.

Positive affirmations boost your confidence and help maintain a good attitude. I learned it takes five positive statements to override one negative statement. Flood your mind with positive statements, quotes, or affirmations throughout the day, every day, to change a negative attitude or to maintain a positive attitude.

Confidence isn't the lack of fear; it is doing what needs to be done despite your fear.

Positive Attitude Challenge

It is nearly impossible to keep a negative attitude while filling up on positive quotes and affirmations. Take the following Attitude Challenge. Over the next forty days, read and focus on one of the listed attitude quotes every day.

Write the quote in a journal in the morning. Meditate on it and apply it as much as possible to situations that arise throughout the day. Before turning in for the night, record the impact the quote had on your day. What happened, when you applied the quote, and when you thought about the quote? At the end of each week, reflect on the quotes you used that week. When the forty days are over, record the change you notice in your overall attitude.

40 Quotes

- All that we are is the result of what we have thought. The mind is everything. What we think, we become.
  ~Anonymou
- They can because they think they can.
  ~Virgil
- If you want to change your life, change your mind.
  ~ Anonymous
- There are no menial jobs, only menial attitudes.
  ~William Bennett
- The pessimist sees difficulty in every opportunity; the optimist sees the opportunity in every difficulty.
  ~Winston Churchill
- Don't ever perceive other people's success as your own failure.
  ~Rob Liano

- Smile when it hurts most.

  ~Anonymous

- The more a mind thinks upon something, the deeper it will take root and affect all subsequent and related thoughts.

  ~A.J. Darkholme

- Your attitude, not your aptitude, will determine your altitude.

  ~Zig Ziglar

- When you think your life is falling apart, it's usually falling together in disguise.

  Charlotte Eriksson

- Life is like a mirror and will reflect back to the thinker what he thinks into it.

  ~Anonymous

- Attitude is your acceptance of the natural laws or your rejection of the natural laws.

  ~Jim Rohn

- Ability is what you're capable of doing. Motivation determines what you do. Attitude determines how well you do it.

  ~Anonymous

- The life each of us lives is the life within the limits of our own thinking. To have life more abundant, we must think in limitless terms of abundance.

  ~Thomas Dreier

- Our attitude toward life determines life's attitude towards us.

  ~Anonymous

- We cannot think of being acceptable to others until we have first proven acceptable to ourselves.
  ~Malcolm De Chazal

- I cannot do everything, but I will not let what I cannot do interfere with what I can do.
  ~Anonymous

- The quality of our expectations determines the quality of our actions.
  ~ Andre Godin

- The mind is everything; what you think, you become.
  ~Anonymous

- Excellence is not a skill. It is an attitude.
  ~Ralph Marston

- Nothing can stop the man with the right mental attitude from achieving his goal; nothing on earth can help the man with the wrong mental attitude.
  ~Anonymous

- The more a mind thinks upon something, the deeper it will take root and affect all subsequent and related thoughts.
  ~A.J. Darkholme

- The life each of us lives is the life within the limits of our own thinking. To have life more abundant, we must think in limitless terms of abundance.
  ~Anonymous

- The greatest day in your life and mine is when we take total responsibility for our attitudes. That's the day we truly grow up.
  ~John C. Maxwell

- As the wheel follows the ox behind, we will become what our thoughts have made us.

  ~Anonymous

- Attitudes are more important than facts.

  ~Karl A. Menninger

- The highest possible stage in moral culture is when we recognize that we ought to control our thoughts.

  ~ Anonymous

- The greatest discovery of my generation is that man can alter his life simply by altering his attitude of mind.

  ~William James

- Nothing great was ever achieved without enthusiasm.

  ~Anonymous

- The only disability in life is a bad attitude.

  ~Scott Hamilton

- If you can't change your fate, change your attitude.

  ~Anonymous

- I can't change the direction of the wind, but I can adjust my sails to always reach my destination.

  ~Jimmy Dean

- How we think shows through in how we act. Attitudes are mirrors of the mind. They reflect thinking.

  ~David Joseph Schwartz

- Attitude is a little thing that makes a big difference.

  ~Winston Churchill

- I've learned from experience that the greater part of our happiness or misery depends on our dispositions and not on our circumstances.

  ~Martha Washington

- To different minds, the same world is a hell and a heaven.

  ~Ralph Waldo Emerson

- I've always believed that you can think positive just as well as you can think negative.

  ~Sugar Ray Robinson

- It is the attitude that drives everyone's thinking. If one can control his or her attitude, he/she will succeed in Life.

  ~Anonymous

- The words I am . . . are potent words; be careful what you hitch them to. The thing you're claiming has a way of reaching back and claiming you.

  ~ A.L. Kitselman

- We cannot think of being acceptable to others until we have first proven acceptable to ourselves.

  ~ Malcolm De Chaz

CHAPTER FOURTEEN

Smile Often, Laugh Out Loud

Leave a Lasting Impression

"Life is a first impression. You get one shot at it. Make it everlasting."

~J.R. Rim

There is a saying, "You never get a second chance to make a good first impression." First impressions are exactly that, the impression you leave the first time you encounter or interact with someone. You can make a first impression only once, however, you can always make a conscious effort to leave a lasting positive impression. This allows you to take control over the way you want to be remembered.

An immediate way to leave a positive impression is to flash the pearly whites. In other words, smile as stated in chapter seven. A smile can be the initial ice breaker when meeting someone. It can communicate warmth, trustworthiness, and friendliness. Smiling may reduce the tension, and uncertainty of meeting individuals for the first time. It says, "Welcome to my world." Smiling has been mentioned before, but it is worth mentioning again and again due to the powerful impact something as simple as a smile can have when interacting with another individual.

Another way to leave a lasting impression is to laugh. Don't take yourself too seriously. When you can laugh at yourself, others will relax around you and laugh too. If you don't laugh at yourself once in a while, you run the risk of being labeled rigid or cold. You definitely don't want to leave that impression or foster such a reputation.

Taking time to serve others is an excellent opportunity to leave a lasting impression. Look around; as you do, observe the many ways to serve someone else. As you settle into your role and responsibilities, don't forget to lend a helping hand whenever possible. Try not to restrict being of service to the immediate team, but don't spread yourself too thin either. Be strategic, and select the times you serve wisely.

The simple acts of being kind and using manners will transform the way you are perceived and also leave a positive impression. Be polite. Say please, thank you, and apologize when appropriate to do so.

This is how the foundation for becoming the icon is laid. What legacy do you want to leave? Your actions will speak louder than any words that ever come out of your mouth.

Although your goal is not to subject anyone to comparison on purpose, you do want to leave such a positive impact within the organization that when it is time to move on, your legacy will be one of excellence and quality service to others. Your lasting impression will be the one who was well-liked, well-known, and well-respected, the icon. You will be the person the phrase, "You've got some big shoes to fill," refers to.

Resources

- You may find the resources, bibliography, etc. cited in this book on my website: www.bettyjewellslater.com.
- You may also go there to subscribe and share your experience with the focus methods in chapter five.
- A companion journal to the 40-Day Attitude Challenge in chapter thirteen can be found there as well.

About the Author

Producer. Coach. Actor. Speaker. Author

Betty Jewell Slater is helping people become Kingdom Influencers. She is an award-winning film producer, a coach, actor, speaker, and author who helps individuals, organizations, and actors identify and break through limiting systems and beliefs, so they can experience unhackability, become all they were created to be, and impact the kingdom of God in their niche all over the world. She lives in the San Francisco Bay area and has one adult son, William.

Connect with her at BettyJewellSlater.com

A Fresh Approach to Public Speaking

Betty provides a fresh approach to public speaking by presenting in costume as one of the following matriarchs of history

Invite Betty to speak: BettyJewellSlater.com

Mrs. Coretta Scott King

Harriet Tubman

Mrs. Rosa Parks

Bessie Coleman

Take your leadership skills to the next level

Are You Operating at Your Fullest Potential as a Leader?

Take the Free assessment at the site below

TheUnhackableLeader.com

THE UNHACKABLE
LEADER

*Are You an Actor? Do You Want to Act?
Are You Getting Roles?*

Learn the **5** Critical Acting Skills You Need to Land Big Roles!

BettyJewellSlater.com

30 Days to Close the Gap Between Faith and Fear

Learn More

BettyJewellSlater.com/unhackable

The #1 Speaker Development Program for Women

Speaking is about fulfilling your purpose, changing lives, and gaining confidence while serving others. I can help you Unlock Your voice, Unlock Your Confidence, Unlock Your Healing and
UNLEASH YOUR PURPOSE

StageTherapyWithBettyJewellSlater.com